T0065501

The Expectations of Our Standards

*Do You Know What You Want
Out of This Relationship*

EARLYSHIA O. THOMAS

WESTBOW
PRESS°
A DIVISION OF THOMAS NELSON
& ZONDERVAN

WestBow Press books may be ordered through booksellers or by contacting:

WestBow Press
A Division of Thomas Nelson & Zondervan
1663 Liberty Drive
Bloomington, IN 47403
www.westbowpress.com
844-714-3454

ISBN: 978-1-6642-3525-0 (sc)
ISBN: 978-1-6642-3524-3 (e)

Print information available on the last page.

WestBow Press rev. date: 05/28/2021

CONTENTS

CONTENTS

ACKNOWLEDGEMENTS

First and foremost, thank God for blessing me with numerous gifts to reach His people! Without Him I have surely found that I am NOTHING, but with Him there is nothing that I cannot do! To a special woman, who is no longer with me in the natural, but I feel her everyday; my mom Belinda (B.B.)Thomas. Thank you for pushing me toward dreams I never imagined. You never said no when I asked to be a part of something or go somewhere that would benefit my educational, professional, and social endeavors. I am thankful each day that I was blessed with a mother who gave of herself, selflessly, in every aspect of my life. My love for you will never die, nor will the memories we've shared. Here's to another accomplishment! Tell my Granny I miss her and I am trying my best to make you two proud!

Some people aren't fortunate to have siblings. I was, however, lucky enough to have the awesome opportunity to share this life with a twin! Earl, yes, his name is really Earl, you are my inspiration. Everyone says I have drive, but your ambition is what motivates me to do what I do. Keep living your dreams Pastor! The world will know you soon! To my other siblings: Romona, Jay, and Vashawn (Bubba), thank you for supporting the things that I do. I love y'all even though sometimes I don't express it enough. I'd like to send a special shout out to my nieces and nephews! You all are my kids! Everything I do, I do for you to know that there is nothing in life that can stop you from reaching your goals. One day, you will understand the methods to my madness, but until then keep on loving me! To my late father, who transitioned earlier this year, thank you for supporting me, even when you didn't understand the things I wanted to do. I know that my work ethic and drive to succeed comes from you. To my Aunties and God-Mother, you all stepped up and stepped in when I needed you most. Even as an adult I couldn't navigate some of the things in my life without you and I am deeply grateful for your love.

To the greatest friends in the entire world: Mary, Ranae, Ches, Carmen, Paula, Franky, April, Tasha, Lori, Jamie, Rodesia, Danyelle, MaShundra, Tora, and Nancy! I couldn't ask for a more supportive group of people in my corner! No matter what it is, how long it takes, or how far apart we are, there is NOTHING I can't ask of you. Thank you for being who you are and loving me. To the Dallas Alumnae Chapter of Delta Sigma Theta Sorority, Incorporated and my Talented and Gifted Line Sistas, (Century 9 E.I.T.), words cannot express how grateful I am to have you in my life. At a time when God knew I needed strong shoulders to lift me up, He brought me you. I am forever thankful to be a member of the greatest sorority in the world!

To the New Mt. Zion P.B. C., you were my foundation and I thank you for your continuous support throughout every accomplishment I have obtained. My mentors: Dr. Creslond Fannin, Myishia Gray, and Chyrel Roseborough; thank you for taking me under your wings and providing me with the knowledge and skills to become the woman I am now. Mrs. Verna Mitchell and Dr. Andrea Hilburn, you two were my first role models! I would not be who I am as an educator without your guidance and support. I hope to be to some little Black girl searching for her place in life, what you were, and still are to me. A special thank you to Dr. Maurice Williams, Jr. and Christopher Hill for inspiring me to finish what I started! To those whom I may not have mentioned, please know that I thank and love you as well. I could not have made it this far without you, and I look forward to sharing even more great achievements with you in the future!

A NOTE FROM THE AUTHOR

Let me first start by saying I am super excited to share my thoughts with you! I've always wanted to write a book, but didn't know exactly what to write about. As an English teacher, I am reading and writing every day, therefore, I knew whatever I wrote about had to be good!

This book was actually created from a casual conversation I had with one of my former co-workers! One day I was leaving campus, and I'm still unsure of how we began discussing the topic, but I remember telling her something to the effect that we as women have to realize that our standards and expectations are not the same things. That was years ago and I am now sharing my concept of *The Expectations of Our Standards*.

Please know that these are just my thoughts. I am not trying to preach to you or even convince you to believe what I do. I simply wanted to share with you what I've been contemplating and why sometimes relationships may not work out the way we plan. I hope you enjoy reading my thoughts as much as I enjoyed writing them.

THE CONCEPTION

The Expectations of Our Standards was conceived during a conversation I once had with my former co-worker about relationships. While I'm not exactly sure what we were discussing and how the concept came up, I am definitely glad I made the comment about us, as women, knowing the difference between our expectations and our standards.

I am in no way trying to push my thoughts and/or beliefs off onto anyone. I do, however, want you to truly analyze the text and make a few conscious decisions about your relationships. Furthermore, I'd like for you to examine what is being said and think about what you can do to understand yourself and your (future) mate more critically.

As I composed each chapter, you will see that I reference several things, specifically my experiences. I wrote from my heart and asked myself those questions that many women have about why our relationships never seem to work out the way envisioned. Every chapter is a chapter that I know every reader can relate to. This book is specifically geared toward young women, ages 25-40. I selected this demographic because during those ages women tend to find out exactly who they are and if they don't know, they are searching for what they want in a mate. However, this is a good read for anyone!

I hope you enjoy The Expectations of Our Standards as much as I loved writing it. Share with me your comments and feedback at:

Earlyshia O. Thomas
P.O. Box 763444
Dallas, TX 75376

or

mss_thomas32@gmail.com

Happy Reading!

PRE-PONDERANCE

1. Do you feel you are ready for a relationship? Explain why.

2. What type of mate do you attract? Think about two of the people you've dated, list their characteristics (i.e. career, knows God, college degree, etc.).

3. What are your top 3 standards?

   a.
   b.
   c.

4. What does the selection of your mate say about your standards as a woman?

5. What are your top 3 expectations of your mate?

6. How do your previous relationships directly affect the relationships you have now?

7. If you are in a relationship, where did you meet your mate? If you are not in a relationship, what places do you usually meet men?

ONE

The Standard vs. The Expectation

As women, we often confuse our standards with our expectations. They definitely correlate with one another; however, they are unquestionably separate components when discussing relationships. Simply, your standard is what you require and your expectation is the attitude of what you hope will be done for him to continue to meet your standards. Usually when someone says *your standards are too high,* it means the person either does not have any or they simply don't meet them. Don't let that bother you. When you maintain your standards, your potential mate will either rise to the challenge or walk away because he cannot. If they walk, let them. They were not what you needed anyway.

Have you ever thought about what you want in a mate? Of course, we all have thought about the type of man we will marry one day. Yet, when we make that list of standards, we realize that we really don't know what we want. Before reading this chapter, you were asked to list your top three standards. These may have ranged from having a career and being established, to not living with his mom and having more than one "baby mama"! These are our standards. For me, I need a protector and a provider. Make me feel safe and make sure I will always have a roof over my head. We can work on the rest together. One other top standard I have is a man has to make me feel special; like I'm the only woman in the world made just for him. He needs to love me more than I love him! This is what I look for in a man when he is courting me. The question I ask myself as we are getting to know each other is what did he do to grasp my attention and make me feel like I was the only woman in the world he noticed and wanted to get to know? This is a requirement that I will never minimize because I do something to make me feel special every day. Whether it's putting on make-up, styling my hair a different way, buying a new outfit, or taking myself out to dinner; I make me feel like there is nothing I cannot do or have every day of the week, and that is how I want my man to make me feel.

My cousin has always told me that I can't expect others to do what I would do. In a relationship, we cannot expect a man to do what we would do, especially if we don't communicate our expectations. I dated a guy that texted me good morning every morning. I felt like I was the first person he thought about when he woke up; and this made me feel so special! That text made even the worse of mornings better. Being who I am, I would expect my next insignificant other, someone I am just dating, to do the same. Of course, I would need to communicate this to him, as this is an expectation of mine. This differs from my standard of him, "having to make me feel special", because now I expect him to take what I have conversed with him about and put it into action. It doesn't have to be a text that he sends. It could be a rose on my pillow each Monday morning, or an email at lunch time to let me know that he's thinking of me. I guess what I'm trying to say is my expectation is an attitude of anticipation. It's something that I am looking forward to because it says he listens when I speak and cares about what I say. What are your expectations of your mate? Revisit the pre-reading questions and see if your answer now differs.

TWO

Where You Meet Him

One thing I admire about men is they will meet their woman exactly where she is, and help her rise to the status of potential he saw in her when they first met. Women typically don't want a project when it comes to finding "Prince Charming". There is this unrealistic concept that is embedded in our minds that the man we will get will already have himself pulled together. WRONG! The reality is we all need work and when we meet our mate we have to learn to meet him where he is. This doesn't mean lower your standards, it means don't be so caught up in making sure this man fits that particular standard to perfection, that you miss out on a good thing. How do you determine a good thing? A good thing can be defined as a man who is gainfully employed, self-sufficient, treats you well and knows exactly how to keep a smile on your face. This isn't to say that he does not have flaws; it just means that he is willing to work around them to keep his woman happy. Keep the requirement; however, make sure you are flexible in seeing his potential to rise to or above the standard. Meet him where he is, then encourage him as he progresses toward where it is he is seeking to be. In this, though, make sure you are not trying to rush his process and that you're being supportive, not authoritative.

There are two folds in talking about where you meet your man. We've discussed the emotive element; now let's talk about the actual component of where you meet your mate. Think about this... It's a nice day around 12:30pm and you decide to stop in Taco Bell to get lunch. You notice the guy who is working the drive-thru checking you out. Automatically, you've judged him. Let's be honest, you did! In your mind, you are saying, "I'm not talking to any man that works at Taco Bell and he works the drive-thru! No ma'am, not me." While you are waiting on your food another customer has a complaint and demands to see the manager. He walks to the counter and says, "I'm the *owner*, how can I help you?" Immediately, your radar is up and you're hoping he's still interested. This should teach you not to be so quick to jump to conclusions about a man's status just because of where you meet him. The fact that he's the owner, and working the drive-thru isn't beneath him, should tell you that he's not only down to earth, but he believes in keeping those around him happy. Honestly, we appreciate our supervisors more when they are assisting us, than when they just sit back and tell us what to do. Stop judging and be open to potential.

Now, there are several happy hour socials that are held throughout the week. Women crowd these places trying to meet that ideal man. It doesn't matter that they are just there to unwind from a grueling day at the office. You want to make sure you're in the right place, at the right time in the event he decides today is the day he wants to look for Mrs. Right. His BMW 750 is parked in valet, he's picked up a round for you and your girls, but he reeks of arrogance and hasn't stopped talking about himself since he sat down. Seriously, is this really the type of man you want? If you are completely honest with yourself, you'd say no. This superficial belief that men with money and nice cars are the men to have is why the great guys working at Burger King are often overlooked. While where you meet him can give you some type of outlook on where things may lead, don't let it define the man and who he can be to you in the future.

Where you meet your mate can say a lot about the type of relationship you are looking for. You've been asked before, "What types of places do you go to meet men?" Take a moment to think about where you go to meet men. Don't let that define the relationship though. Use this as insight in your approach to the relationship you will eventually have.

THREE

It's Just a Number: Age, Credit, Income, Kids, and Zip Code

Age

Let's say you are a forty-year-old woman, dating a twenty-eight-year-old man; society will call you a cougar! A cougar is a woman who dates men much younger than she is. Why does this label bother most women? See, I have no problem with dating a younger man. Therefore, I can definitely relate to the seemingly wild side of the life that alleged cougars live! My advice, however, is to embrace it. These are the best times of your life! Then again, a forty-year old man can date a twenty-eight-year-old woman and society says forty is the new thirty! What is the difference in the two scenarios? Does age really matter in a relationship? When people think about age in a relationship they are concerned with what others think. There was something that attracted you to this person before age became a factor.

Don't let a man's age completely cut him out of the picture. There are some thirty-year-old men who have accomplished more in their lives, than a fifty-year old man who is still trying to find himself. Now this doesn't make him qualified to be your potential mate, but it is a great standard to have in what you are looking for. Now, the fifty-year old man can keep believing fifty is the new forty and that he has time, but that will be all he has in the end! Furthermore, don't reject a younger man because of what society says. I like to say, "While we're worrying about what society is saying about our life, society is happy and living their life!" Are you going to let someone else dictate your happiness or will you allow this man, regardless of his age, show you what happiness means when it is right?

On the contrary, some women, like me, don't like to date men who are much older than them. For personal reasons, in which we'll discuss in the next chapter, I just don't find older men attractive. In reality, it has nothing to do with the physical aspect of an older man, but more with the mental piece. The conversation is different, and the backgrounds are different. There is nothing we'd be able to talk about because our lives will possibly be in two different areas at the time we meet.

As a relatively young woman, although I'm in my late thirties, a man who has been married and has children just doesn't appeal to me. I remember my pastor telling me I'm going to marry a man at least ten years my senior. If I could have called him a lie in the house of the Lord I would have! Some young women flock to men that are older than them. He seems to be a pillar of security because most likely he's established in his career and ready to settle down. This is the perfect man for some women. Don't be afraid to embrace this man, he is not the enemy. He may be exactly what you want and need. However, don't be so skeptical of the young man; he may be just what you've been asking for all along. Just because he is young doesn't mean he can't be your knight in shining armor, who will rescue you from this sea of worthless men you've been battling. Get your man girl!

Credit

You are defined by your credit score in today's society. With bad credit you are limited to the things you can do. A popular rap artist, Lil Boosie, has a song entitled "Independent Women". In it he states, "You ain't a bad chick if you got bad credit". Does the same hold true for a man? Will you date a man with bad credit? Would you actually get rid of a potential mate because of their credit worthiness? A credit score of 568 doesn't necessarily outweigh a great career and the ability to provide for the household. Or does it? Now if you have bad credit and he has bad credit, someone needs to invest in some credit counseling! Nevertheless, you can work with this obstacle. This is a goal maybe both of you can work toward and achieve together in your relationship. Credit does matter; however, know that there are some things that can be done to get you to where you need to be in order to live a great life with a great partner. Although it will be tough, it is definitely attainable without having great credit. What's more, you have to be ready to accept the challenges that come along with it. It's nothing that you can't get through if you work together with the goal of being in a different place in your relationship and personal ambitions.

Income

According to some, God created a woman to be a help mate to her husband. From what we are taught about the Bible, man was created in God's image to provide, protect, and procreate. Will you marry a man that makes less money than you? **STOP!** Before you leap into your explanation of why you wouldn't, think about why you would. I'll give you a few minutes to jot down your reasons... ok now if your reasons of why you wouldn't outweigh your reasons of why you would go back to the drawing board and re-evaluate what you really want in a man.

I once was told that most women want a man to bring certain things to a relationship, but they don't bring half of what they're asking for to the table themselves. This includes finances; both his and yours. There is no doubt that women hustle (get on the move about handling business) and will make it happen for her well-being. However, there are some women who will not be with a man that makes less money than her for several reasons. This could possibly be a fear of not feeling as if she has a *"man's man"*. A *"man's man"* is a man who takes care of home emotionally, physically, spiritually, and financially. Specifically speaking on the financial aspect, he has a career, excellent benefits, and is a provider. Aren't we all looking for this type of man? Do we not all want a man that can provide in every aspect of our lives within our relationship? Not to mention, he makes his woman feel special and puts it down in the bedroom! Nevertheless, when women find this type of man, yet, he makes considerably less than her when it comes to salary, she sometimes makes the wrong decisions regarding her relationship with him. What do you do then? Let him go or keep find a way to work through your own demons in this situation?

The most precise example I can apply is the development of the relationship between Taraji P. Henson and Michael Easley in Steve Harvey's, *Think Like a Man* movie. Taraji was the epitome of the contemporary career woman looking for her equal. Still, in the midst of that, she was also looking for a man that made her feel like a woman. His income bracket didn't fit the bill, but he made her feel safe, emotionally secure, and sexy. What she saw in him was potential. With potential comes the possibility of growing into that multifaceted man that will eventually make the money you know he can make. Is this enough for you? Are you willing to look past where a man is at the moment you meet him and see where he could possibly be with a little encouragement and support from his women? More specifically, can you look past the money "he" makes and look at the money "*we*" make? When you enter a relationship, you give up *me* for *we*, therefore, take a sincere look at the expectations of your standards to be the woman who is going to support your mate and not discourage his efforts because of his fiscal state.

Kids

There was a time when I was holding out for a man that did not have any kids. I'm still that woman! I'd like to say that I still maintain that standard. However, I'm flexible, or at least I'd like to be, in saying the guys I date can only have one child. Does the number of kids a man have matter when seeking a future with him? Of course! As a single woman with no children, you may not fully comprehend the bond between a parent and child. Because of this, there could be tension in a relationship when both parties aren't in agreement with the upbringing of children when the relationship takes a more permanent arrangement. What I may think about raising a child would be overlooked because of my lack of being a biological mother. Yet, when I enter into a relationship with a man who has children, especially if they live with him, my opinion is going to have to be appreciated in some form.

How many kids are too many kids for a man to have? More than two is too many for me! As a woman with no children I feel I am entitled to make the decision on whether or not I want to date a man with children. My personal outlook on this subject is, when I get pregnant, I want the father of my child and myself to go through the expectancy process together, as first-time parents. Call me selfish, and I'll be that, but I just don't want too many other things taking my man's attention away from me. Let's be honest, kids do that! When a woman needs something from her significant other and he has to make the choice on whether he is going to honor her request or the request of his child, a real woman wouldn't want him to do anything else, but take care of his child. In this instance, would I be upset? Maybe for about an hour! I'm spoiled, so sue me. Then again, I couldn't really be upset because I would expect him to do the same for our child if the shoe were on the other foot. Who doesn't like a man that provides for his children? And as a woman, I would hope that you would appreciate that this man you call your mate takes responsibility for his children, even if it means you have to go without.

This question on the number of kids a man has can go on and on forever. There are various opinions and perspectives. When you are faced with the possibility of being in this situation please take into consideration all factors in the circumstance. His having children could turn out to be a blessing in disguise. You could be one that can't conceive and his children could become the children you would have never been able to have. Moreover, you never know if you'd be that mother for his children that they've longed for. Nonetheless, this subject of men with kids varies in opinions and quite frankly just depends on the person. We all have our standards and shouldn't be ashamed in keeping them in tact if that is the way we truly feel.

<u>Zip Code</u>

The old cliché says, "It's not where you come from, but where you're going." How true is that? Unconsciously, women think about where a man comes from. His background plays an important part in her decision to date him. It's kind of similar to the type of woman a guy looks for; a lady in the street, but something else in the bed. Some women seek a man that's corporate, but has some swag (the confidence in which a man carries himself). In my opinion, confidence is one of the sexiest attributes a man can possess. This tells a woman that he is not afraid to take charge when needed and he will take care of her. Also, it tells a woman if she will be able to control her man if he lacks confidence in himself. This is a non-negotiable for me. I'm a strong woman; therefore, my man must have great confidence in himself. It's number two in my top three standards and I am not changing that!

A woman has to feel protected by her significant other. Therefore, she looks for the smart guy that comes from the rough neighborhood. He may have been transported to the magnet school, but he can definitely hold his own with the boys from the neighborhood. Also, he may have gone to the school in his rough neighborhood, but graduated at the top of his class and went on to make something of himself. He could be neither of these things and is just a man from the wrong side of the tracks with a 9-5 and treats you right. I guess what I'm trying to say is it really doesn't matter where a man comes from when it comes to him protecting you. Whether he is a man who rocks a suit on Wall Street or works in a factory in a jumper, if he makes you feel safe when you're with him then he is the perfect man for you.

Let's face it ladies, the type of guy that our friends and

family think we're going to end up with is not the guy we're going to fall in love with. In Tyler Perry's *Daddy's Little Girls*, Gabrielle Union's character fell for a guy with three kids, from a rough neighborhood, body filled with tattoos, and worked as a mechanic. Yet, she didn't let where he came from or what he did at the moment dictate her fate. Instead, she looked past what was presented before her and met him where he was at the time. She then, indirectly, encouraged him to become what she knew he could by supporting him. So, wouldn't you say it is truly not where a man comes from that will determine his outcome in life, but his willingness and potential to become the man a woman needs.

FOUR

Let's Be Clear: It's Not What You Say, But How You Say It

When dating, you have to be clear in every aspect of the relationship you are working towards. The guessing game is never an enjoyable game to play. At times people expect others to read their minds and do what they would do. That is definitely not the case in a relationship. For this reason, open lines of communication are extremely important. Furthermore, the way communication is transmitted is very important. Being up front in letting your mate know what you are seeking in the relationship is valuable. It sets your standard for him and for you. Besides, when you clearly communicate your expectations for the relationship, it leaves no room for your mate to question what it is you want.

Some people use sarcasm as a tactic of "let me hurt you before you hurt me". While everyone should watch how they talk to others, how you speak to your mate is particularly essential. Additionally, what you say is just as important. Growing up, my pastor always said when he's not upset with his wife, she's baby...honey...sweetheart; and when he's upset with her she's still baby...honey...sweetheart. As a child, I didn't get the concept of what he was saying. Now, however, I plainly see that what I say to my mate has a direct reflection on how I see our relationship. If I call him out of his name then obviously,

I see our relationship as something derogatory and offensive, which is a direct reflection on how I perceive our union. This in turn, will also be how others perceive it as well.

On the contrary, if you allow your man to be disrespectful to you, he is also disrespecting your relationship as well. This now speaks volumes about your standards, as well as your expectations. Never let a man tell you who you are. You should already know! If you don't know who you are, then you need to find yourself before you try to immerse yourself in a relationship. Without knowing who you are, how can you effectively be a part of an entity of two people who are trying to build something? Knowing yourself governs how you communicate and how you allow yourself to be communicated to.

Nonverbal communication is just as effective as verbal. What you don't say speaks volumes. The atmosphere you create comes from what you have not said. Think about at time you walked into a room and immediately you felt uncomfortable. No one said anything to you, but their body language and facial expressions made you feel like you should be anywhere, but there. This can also happen in your relationship and you don't even realize it. You walk into the house and don't speak. Your mate may be thinking, "What did I do now?" and you didn't even open your mouth. This form of negative non-verbal communication can be detrimental to a relationship. The effort you put into communicating effectively vocally, you should do so in your actions. The topic of communication could go on and on, but I think we hear enough about that and quite honestly, still don't do it.

The moral of the story is being clear in what you want. Don't continue to play a cat and mouse game with a man who you know isn't going to give you what you desire. He is letting you know, verbally or non-verbally, exactly where you stand in his life. But don't be so uptight in your demands that you're not flexible in what he is willing to give. He's not perfect and won't even attempt to be... even for you! Likewise, you should let your words and actions coincide with one another. Don't say one thing and do another. As the old saying goes, say what you mean and mean what you say. In this, let your actions depict what it is you have said. Communication is the key to any relationship. Don't let the lack of it taint what could possibly become beautiful union.

FIVE

Daddy Issues

The first man most women give their hearts to are their fathers. When a woman's father breaks her heart, what man actually stands a chance at restoring it to love again? While it's highly possible, it is a quite difficult task to undertake. The good news is there are still some men up for the challenge. This man understands your dilemma and is committed to helping you move past your pain. Knowing this, who wouldn't love this man?

I had deep rooted daddy issues. I could never understand how things went downhill at a crucial time in my life. Transitioning from elementary to middle school is an impactful time in a child's life. I won't disclose full details, but know that my daddy shattered my heart and only God was able to repair this vessel. My dad's actions destroyed my faith in men all together. Men were nothing to me! As I grew older, my unrealistic notion was, there was nothing a man could do for me that I couldn't do for myself. Sure, I liked guys and talked to them as a normal teenager would, but I never allowed myself to get emotionally attached to any of my guy friends. Listen, I never allowed myself to get emotionally attached to anyone! No man was ever going to break my heart because I wasn't going to let them. Before you continue reading, think about your relationship, or lack thereof, with your father. How has it shaped you as a woman?

My father eventually apologized, but I still held on to my anger. This was my justification in why I treated men the way I did. I slowly realize that no one was being hurt, but me. Everyone had moved on with their lives and I was still just so angry! At some point, I stopped and realized I wasn't hindering anyone, but myself. While I was still dwelling in my father's past transgressions, living a miserable life, he had moved on and made peace within and was now living the best life he knew how. At that moment, I GOT OVER IT AND MOVED ON! I know it is definitely easier said than done. It took lots of counseling, praying, and discipline, but I made it to a place of healing and forgiveness.

Don't rush the process. It will not happen overnight; in a month; maybe not even a year. The joy is knowing it will happen one day! You can no longer inhabit these ill feelings toward men because of what your father did. Someday you will feel this irresistible peace and at that moment you will exhale every struggle you've endured with every man who's broken your heart, damaged your spirit, and tried to destroy your soul. It is at that time you will truly open yourself to accept the love that has been trying to find you.

Frederick Douglas said, "It is easier to build a strong child than to repair a broken man." There are so many broken women walking around carrying stuff from childhood. One question my friend and I contemplate even now is, "Is it worse for a child to not grow up with a father or for one to grow up with one and he leaves? The answers to this question vary, but the result is still the same; a broken child. These broken little girls, whether they had a father who left or was just never there, grow up to become women who have developed daddy issues. These issues have a profound impact on women's relationships with men. Some suppress their initial feelings and learn to live with the inescapable pain. Others still haven't quite figured out how to deal with the pain and live in the moment of it all their lives.

Would you agree with the statement, "Before you can completely give yourself to a man, you must first take care of your "daddy issues"? I really don't think you can love a man without loving your father to some degree, but that is just my opinion. I'm not saying you have to want your unborn son to be like your daddy like Beyoncé, but you must admit, the man we eventually fall for has some characteristic we admire or loved in our father. In contrast, there may be traits that your father possess that you irrevocably want to forget and hope no man you encounter shares these same qualities. That is perfectly ok. What would it be like to find that man who is abusive… like your father? Or he drinks… like your father? Maybe he doesn't have any ambition… like your father? These are some characteristics that your father possessed that you may want to avoid in your relationship.

Think about the man you are with or you'd like to be with. If he held every great attribute your dad held, wouldn't that be like dating your dad? I'm just saying people do insane things like that every now and then. Seriously, while our dads are the first persons to show us what love looks like, they also show us what it doesn't. No matter whom we end up falling for, the daddy issues must be dealt with. It can make or break your relationship.

SIX

Pride

Webster's Dictionary defines pride as a high regard or inordinate opinion of one's own dignity, importance, merit, or superiority, whether as cherished in the mind or as displayed in conduct. Great opportunities are often hindered because of pride. Some women, particularly African-American women, have this sense of entitlement like someone owes them something. Now don't take offense to what I just said. It's true that women become so caught up in their feelings that they let their pride prevent them from being with a good man.

I'm a very prideful person. I absolutely dislike asking people, especially a man, for anything or making it seem like I need something. In my unrealistic mind, it makes me feel weak. I know; it's utterly insane. Yet, one thing I am not prideful about is admitting when I am wrong. Often time, people concede to a situation entirely too late and the damage has been done. Have you ever experienced a time when you knew you were wrong, but your pride would not let you admit it? Tell me, what you got from holding on to whatever it was that your pride wouldn't let you do or say? Better yet, let's take a moment to discuss what you lost.

Pride is an explicit component of the standards we encompass. It is what keeps our standards at the level that they are. Your pride won't let you "relax" those standards enough to give that guy with three kids a chance. Oh, no ma'am! Geesh, he has three kids! Except, did you examine the fact that these three children were by the same woman, whom he was once married to, and she passed away? Conversely, maybe he and his wife divorced and it was better for the kids to live with their father while they co-parent? It all bars down to what other people think of you and this "situation" you've gotten yourself into. Remember I told you, life is enjoying itself while you are worried about what life is thinking about you. Live honey! You deserve whatever happiness comes your way; even if it is packaged differently than you thought it would come. Often time we get exactly what we've asked for, but because it doesn't come the way we expected, we want to send it back. That's pride ladies! We ask for a provider, but he doesn't have a college degree. Does that necessarily eliminate this man from being able to provide? The package may not come all gift wrapped with a bow, but it is the package you've asked for. Now embrace it, put your pride aside, and love your man!

Something else pride won't let us do is be vulnerable. Sometimes it's ok to let your guard down and let someone in. Think about who is waiting for you when you get home after a long day of work? Who keeps you warm at night on those rainy days, when boo weather (rain or cold weather that is perfect for cuddling) is in full affect? If the answers to these two questions are no one, maybe the reason you don't have this is because your pride won't let you. The advantage of being in a relationship is being able to be vulnerable with your man. Being able to make mistakes and admit your faults go along ways in a relationship. Pride keeps you from doing this. Moreover, pride stops you from taking chances that could change your destiny. Don't be afraid to put your pride aside, as the old folks say, and go after what you want. In the end, your happiness is what is most important.

Now don't be confused; notice in the definition it states pride is *one's* opinion of importance of not only everyone else, but of yourself. With that being said, have some pride in yourself! Take pride in what you bring to the table; whatever that may be. I'm a plus sized woman, and you can believe that I am the finest plus sized woman that walks the Earth! My sexy is beautiful honey! I know who I am and I know what I offer a man. I won't get super spiritual , but I will say this, know who created you and that He would not have created anything less than in His own image. If you can't have pride in anything else, have some in that notion.

SEVEN

His Hurt

By nature, women are emotional creatures. I don't think women realize, men are just as emotional as they are. Their gift, however, is being able to control their emotions and operate in reason. Being so emotionally caught up in past hurts, some women often forget about an essential element that has great significance in the idea of relationships: *his hurt.*

What is "his hurt"? I'm glad you asked! His hurt is just as fragile as yours. His hurt is trust issues, baby mama drama, lack of a positive male role model, his father leaving him, or his mom not spending time with him. His hurt is fighting to prove his manhood, not only to society, but to his woman. His hurt is working daily to provide for his family and coming home to an empty house wondering what he will eat for dinner. His hurt is finding out the woman he loves and plans to spend the rest of his life with is cheating on him and shattering the heart he so freely gave to her. Furthermore, he may feel he will never measure up to the man others wanted him to be, even when he continues to strive to be the best man he knows how, is his hurt. His hurt! His hurt! His hurt! It can be quite insensitive of women to only consider their feelings in a relationship when often times we are the motivating factor of his hurt.

Sometimes it is forgotten that the same man who women like to place blame on for hurting them can just as well charge a woman for damaging his faith in relationships. It is imperative for us to remember that men are human also. As much as we'd like to overlook the truism that men are powerful beings who should know how to manage the chaos that arises in their lives, we must also grasp the concept that he can become overwhelmed in the aspect of a relationship as well. Someone so caught up in their own hurt may unconsciously not recognize another person's hurt. It is often said that hurt people, hurt people. After I've been hurt a few times, I would want someone to feel my pain! On the other hand, I can't whole heartedly agree with the statement above. I believe hurt people are seeking comfort in others that they cannot find within themselves. It doesn't necessarily mean that because they are hurt, they want to hurt others. It could simply mean that their hurt is what drives them into the arms of someone who understands what they are feeling at the moment. You may question why should you even care about his hurt? Well you should care because he cared about your hurt. Again, selfishly, some women think that they are the only ones who have ever been hurt in a relationship. Now they expect every man to in some shape, form, or fashion hurt them. Your standards will dictate the type of man you allow to come into your life. Unfortunately, if you have not re-evaluated them after your failed relationships, then you will continue to attract and be hurt by the same types of men.

Men know that they have, at some point in their lives, hurt a woman. They own up to it and rationalize that because they have been hurt, this is why they've at some point hurt someone else. Whether his hurting another woman was intentional or not, this is now your chance to help restore confidence in this man, who will potentially be your mate, and support him, past his wounds. You have to show him now that you can love him past his discomfort and be the difference he is looking for in his mate. He now has a certain standard that he is seeking and what he seeks does not reflect what has hurt him. Yet, it replicates your standards.

As we close this chapter, I want to emphasize the significance of observing your reaction to his hurt. Please don't discount the fact that he's been hurt in the past. Now sometimes women can act as if they are the only ones who have ever been hurt. Daddy issues may slightly have something to do with this. Nonetheless, at some point women have to stop holding their significant others to the same standard as they've held their father. I have been guilty of viewing the men in my life "hurts" as less significant than mine. I didn't realize that I was hurting my relationships, not helping them develop with this type of thinking. The response of irrelevance to a man's brokenness may as well be a slap in the face to his masculinity. Real men do cry and they need a real woman's shoulder to cry on when the moment presents itself.

EIGHT

Just Listen

Most people listen with the intent of responding. Have you ever stopped and listened to what it is your mate was actually saying to you? One of the greatest gifts we were blessed with was the skill of listening. It is such a joy to meet someone who just listens. We always hear that communication is one of the most important aspects of a relationship. Sometimes, however, it is what you don't say that has the greatest impact. Just listening can be more beneficial than inserting your opinion; especially an opinion that is not welcomed. It is often stated that we should be quick to listen and slow to speak. I have found this to be true in many ways.

You'd agree that when you are conversing with someone your natural reaction is to listen then respond. At times your mate just needs you to listen. He doesn't need your advice, to tell him what you believe, and definitely not to tell him what he is doing wrong. He just needs you to listen! He needs you to listen to how his day went; or maybe an idea that he's been pondering, but doesn't know where to start. Just being there, giving moral support goes a long way in your relationship. Men typically share their ideas with other men, definitely not their mates. They are fearful of rejection and/or being misunderstood. Therefore, if men do not feel secure enough to come to you for support then you will probably never completely have their reliance in a relationship.

You've heard me mention the phrase "inserting your opinion" earlier in the chapter. This is vital to your relationship. Although we feel like people want our opinion and value what we say, sometimes it is not needed. For instance, your mate comes to you and says he is deciding to pursue a new career opportunity. He is in the midst of sharing with you his aspirations and that he hopes to get this new position. The look on your face, though, says what you can't verbally express. He then asks you, "What do you think babe?" It is my hope that you referred back to chapter four and took a moment to think about your response. We both know that you may want to say what is exactly on your mind, but at a time such as this, he needs your support more than anything. He has already made up his mind about what he is going to do. He isn't looking for your approval, he wants your support. On the other hand, if what he is saying does not sound like it will be beneficial to his future and that of your relationship; it is your obligation to say something. Don't let your need to feel as if you have to help him with this, overshadow the decision he has already made. Remember, he has come to you for support, not for your advice.

Listening can be a difficult task. Yet, it is a skill that can easily be learned. It is in our nature as women to want to be heard. Everything we say has an inspiring belief that we are helping a situation. While this may hold true, when we take a look at a situation, after we have given our opinion, sometimes it is found that we have complicated the situation more. Contrary to popular belief, when people ask for your opinion, they just want you to agree with the decision they have made. They don't really want to know your opinion.

Well, sometimes they do, but most times they just want to be validated in whatever they have decided to embark upon. Repeat after me: I WILL JUST LISTEN! It will definitely strengthen your relationship.

NINE

Qualifying the Unqualified

You've often heard the phrase, "Favor ain't fair." This simply means that when you have the favor of God, He will sometimes allow you to obtain some things that you may not be qualified for. NEWS FLASH... you dear are NOT God! You are in no position to distribute favor. Furthermore, you should really stop trying to qualify these men entering your life who are unqualified to fill the position of being your mate.

*** I want you to stop and take a moment to think about the men who were unqualified, but you try to qualify them. Make a list of what made them unqualified. Think about your standards and expectations at that particular point in your life. Did they or did they not meet the expectations of your standards?

It doesn't take long to realize whether you want to be with someone or not. During this time, you are getting to know the person and trying to figure out exactly what you like and dislike about them. Of course, physically, the person has captured your attention, but it is going to take more than just a sexy smile and a nice body to keep you engaged in the relationship. What sense does it make to give your time to someone who doesn't deserve it? I surveyed twenty women between the ages of eighteen to forty, of various ethnic groups, and asked them what made a man unqualified. Let's take a moment to consider some of the answers they gave on their surveys. *Characteristics which makes a man unqualified to be your potential mate are:*

- **If he is insecure**: Ladies you do not want a man that questions everything you do. If he is insecure before the relationship, trust me, he will be insecure during the relationship.

- **If he does not support your aspirations or endeavors**: Your significant other should always support whatever it is you are wanting to do; even at times when they don't agree with it. If no one else supports your goals and dreams, your mate should.

- **If he does not take care of his children**: A man that does not take care of his children from a previous relationship will not take care of yours. "Why are you different?" you ask. Oh! You're not!

- **If the only time you hear from him is for sex**: A man will spend their time where they want. Therefore, if the only time you hear from this man and end up in bed with him, and that's the only time you hear from him, you are not the one. Not only is he unqualified to be your mate, but he's also unqualified you in that area.

- **If the only time you want this man is for sexual pleasure**: As stated before, women are emotional by nature. Now it has been found that women can have a sexual relationship with a man without attachment. However, eventually women begin to feel some type of connection to this man. It's just in our nature. Stop trying to qualify this man when you know he will never be what you are looking for in a mate. You will never give yourself to him the way a woman should give of themselves to their man. Great sex will never overshadow the characteristics of a great relationship.

Unqualified men will most of the time look as if they meet the standard. They dress well, speak eloquently, and treat you the way a woman should be treated. Nevertheless, it doesn't take long for their flaws to be revealed. By this time, however, you've probably developed feelings for this man and it's hard to let go. When you begin to care about someone it is hard to look past what makes them unqualified. However, when you've had enough of trying to qualify this unqualified individual, you will begin to appreciate your standards and expectations more. Therefore, LET GO of this man who is not remotely close to what you are looking for!!! He is not qualified!

TEN

Take Your Own Advice

Lord knows that it is so hard to take your own advice. Some women always find themselves telling their girlfriends what they need to do, but can never seem to take the same stance in their decision making. When giving or seeking advice, know that you and that person have different standards and expectations. No one accepts or expects the same things. Therefore, you have to be cautious when it comes to who you are taking the advice from. Furthermore, when you are giving the advice, put yourself in the person's shoes that you are giving the advice to. You may be speaking from your own point of view when, in reality, you should be looking at it from their viewpoint.

Have you ever given someone advice and then wish you'd done the same thing when it was you that was in this exact situation? At times, you may feel that it is truly something wrong with you. You just don't get how you can give someone else, in your same situation, the advice you know you should be giving to yourself. Remarkably, we all do this to see how well it works for the person we gave the advice to first. We say to ourselves, "If it works for her, then maybe it'll work for me". Yet, we have that, "I'm glad it was her and not me," attitude when our dear, dejected friend isn't quite so lucky.

Remember I stated that we can't really compare the advice

we give or get when our standards and expectations aren't the same. Think about one of your friends who may be dealing with a similar issue with her mate as you. Look at your top three standards at the beginning of the book and compare them with what you believe her standards are. Do they compare? If so, explain how. If not... then why would you want to receive advice from her when you can't even correlate the paradigms of what you require from your mates?

It's a catch twenty-two when it comes to what you should do in a relationship. While it's always important to be open to the insight from those on the outside looking in, we have to be careful of those who are giving out counsel to discourage, not encourage. Their counsel advises against the bright side of what you hope to achieve in making your relationship work. Furthermore, what is discussed sometimes is never about what you should do to help the relationship, but rather what they would not tolerate in a relationship; therefore, you shouldn't tolerate it either. These friends are always negative and telling you what you need to let go of instead of what you need to work on; whether this is with or without your mate.

Let's take another moment to examine our close friends. Which one is the one who always has something bad to say about your man? Think about when you and your man are not getting along, is she constantly the one telling you to leave or you can do better than him? That is who you do NOT want to take advice from. Now I'm not going to go as far as to say she isn't your friend, but I will say she doesn't know what her standards or expectations are, therefore, she resorts to the negative aspect of relationships. She simply doesn't know how to give the "good" relationship advice because her negative attitude has kept her single.

I often say, "There is only one standard... EXCELLENCE!"

I live by this daily and I expect whomever will be my life to live by this standard also. I don't *expect* them to do as I do, but I do expect that in whatever it is they want to do is done with a spirit of excellence. This is how you have to go about your relationships ladies. Reflect on your current or last relationship (if you're single) and ask yourself what did I do each day that made my mate feel like they were the only person I wanted to be with? Now, ask yourself *how* did I do it? Be honest, did you just send the good morning text because that's what you knew they wanted or because you knew it would bring a smile to their face? Put yourself in their position. How would it feel if they just did things in the relationship because they knew that's what was *expected* and not because they wanted to make you feel proud to be with them? This is also a *take your own advice* teachable moment. If you find yourself just doing things out of habit, consider some new technique to bring some more romance to your relationship! Furthermore, do it with excellence!

POST READING QUESTIONS

1. Are you ready to enter a relationship? Explain why.

2. Have your top 3 standards changed? If so, list them and then explain why. If not, explain why you'd keep them the same.

3. What was the most meaningful chapter of the book for you? Why?

4. If you had to disagree with anything in the bool, what would it be? And why?

5. Have your expectations changed? Why or why not?

6. After reading this book, what is one thing you will change in your relationship or before you enter another relationship (if you're single)?

7. What do you now expect of yourself in a relationship?

Printed in the United States
by Baker & Taylor Publisher Services